Like a River
Edward Mongin

Compiled by Teresa Ann Mongin

© 2023 Edward Mongin
All Rights Reserved

The author and his family would like to take a moment to thank you for your order, it is our greatest hope that you enjoy the pages inside. If you or your family would like a copy of this book go to the link below. May God bless you and bring you peace on your journey through this lovely life.

https://www.amazon.com/dp/B0CQNL4L1Y

TABLE OF CONTENTS

FROM THE EDITOR	8
PART ONE: LOVE	15
HOW I MET MY WIFE	16
IN ALL THE SONGS OF SOLOMON	22
TERESA'S LOVE	23
I LOVE MY WOMAN	24
IT TAKES A LOT OF WATER	25
WHEN THINGS ARE BAD	26
ALL GOOD THINGS TAKE TIME	27
WE MAY BE AS DIFFERENT	28
I STOPPED TO THINK TODAY	29
OUR LOVE IS NOT A STAGNANT POND	30
LOTTERY TICKETS	31
THE MONKEY GREETING CARD	32
BE MY VALENTINE	33
I LOVE YOU IN THE MORNING	34
TWENTY-FIVE	35
TWENTY-SEVEN	36
I'VE BEEN LOOKING	37
TWENTY-NINE	38
I WANT YOU TO KNOW	39

THIRTY	40
TO PLUCK A ROSE	41
A QUIET TIME	42
SOMETIMES INSIDE I FEEL ALONE	43
THIRTY-TWO	44
THE TRUNK OF A TREE	46
YOU DON'T ASK WHY	48
TERESA BE MINE	49
FORTY-TWO	50
PART TWO: FRIENDSHIP	53
BILLY AND HIS 394	54
PETER THE PLINK	56
HALF OVER	58
THE REUNION	60
50 YEARS	61
THE DEVIL'S PLAN	64
ODE TO ANNETTE	67
SISTER DONNA	69
SISTER CHERYL	70
AMY	71
BOOMER'S IN A PLACE WHERE	72
FRANK	73
MISSING THEM	75
DEBBIE AND KEN - A LOVE THAT NEVER ENDS	76

ED AND ROSIE FISHIN'	77
PART THREE: LIFE	80
LIKE A RIVER	81
SEPTEMBER 11TH 2001	83
I CAME TO SEE	85
JOYCE'S HEART	86
MONGIN FAMILY PRAYER	87
MOODS	88
PARENTS' NIGHT	89
LISA	90
TINA'S GIFT	91
ANNIE REA	93
TRENT	95
A FAR AWAY WEDDING WISH	97
LIKE YOUR MOTHER	98
RAINDROPS AND RAINBOWS	99
THE WHALE	101
TURNING FORTY	103
THE PERFECT THIEF	105
LEONE'S POEM	106
A LOOK IN THE MIRROR	107
MY LAST PRAYER	108
PART FOUR: STORIES BEHIND THE POEMS	110
SURPRISE	111

BILLY'S STORY	112
PETER'S STORY	113
REUNION POEMS	114
THE STORIES FOR OUR CHURCH	115
BOOMER'S STORY	116
FRANK'S STORY	118
DEBBIE AND KEN'S WEDDING STORY	119
ED & ROSIE FISHIN	120
JOYCE'S STORY	121
OUR CHILDREN	122
RAINDROPS AND RAINBOWS	123
THE WHALE STORY	124
LEONE'S POEM STORY	125
FAMILY PRAYER STORY	126
MY LAST PRAYER	127
ABOUT THE AUTHOR	129

FROM THE EDITOR

A few weeks before the final edition of this book went to print, its author, my grandfather – almost died.

Edward Mongin is an avid hunter and fisherman, and it's not an exaggeration to say he has spent more of his life in the woods than he ever did at home. In fact, every year our family celebrates Thanksgiving two weeks early so my grandfather can spend most of November who-knows-where hunting deer.

Only four days after our early Thanksgiving celebration, Ed Mongin found himself in the middle of the woods, pinned to the ground by a giant balsam tree blown on top of him in the wind.

His friend immediately ran over, covered him in a jacket, and called for aid. On the surface, this sounds like such a simple thing, but in reality, this was the first of many miracles to unfold.

My grandfather is alone in the middle of nowhere so often that the family mandated he wear a GPS tracker at all times. So, the presence of another person was an absurd circumstance all on its own.

That they also had cell signal in the north woods of Wisconsin was another serendipitous situation, and that Ed ended up with an emergency team who could poke him with an IV from the back of a pick-up truck, take him to an access point for the helicopter, and make the wise recommendation to fly him to the best trauma center in the state – well, my grandfather might say he had a team of angels at his side.

My grandmother, Teresa, along with a handful of family members rushed to the hospital to be at his side only to find that the prognosis was not very positive. The surgeon was unsure if Ed would survive the surgery, and because the tree had totally dislocated several vertebrae in his upper spine, that same surgeon was convinced Ed would never walk again.

A tragic prognosis for a man who valued his independence more than most.

My grandfather is a unique man. His charisma is magnetic as demonstrated by his large circle of friends, all of whom have nicknames based on inside jokes and decades of debauchery.

He is also very connected to his community and beloved by our family, which is really saying something because Edward is sort of a ghostly presence in our lives. He's almost never home and instead has spent almost all of his eighty-some years meandering through the woods hunting, fishing, and constantly negotiating the gray areas in every recreational rule ever written.

Whenever I go back to my hometown to visit my grandparents, I know it's unlikely my grandfather will be home and instead I'll have the honor of spending time with Grandma Teresa.

I usually find her reading from her chair, making something delicious in the kitchen, or on her way out for a walk. She's mastered every gluten-free, dairy-free, vegan, whatever-else-you-need baking hack there is, and her cooking is at the center of every Easter, Thanksgiving, and Christmas – the three holidays that continue to draw her thirty-plus children, grandkids, and great grandkids back home.

My grandparents' house has been homebase ever since I can remember, and even before I can't. As the first born of twelve grandchildren, I spent the first few years of my life living with Ed and Teresa. They were only in their forties at the time, so I've had the privilege of watching them grow together. And in all honesty, they feel more like another set of parents to me.

Perhaps that's why early on Grandpa adorned me with one of his poems and my very first nickname: Filene.

> Filene Mandine Sandine and I
> A fishing we would go
> I taught her how to bait a hook
> I taught her how to throw
>
> She listened to her grandpa
> And learned what life's about
> She sat beside a babbling brook
> And caught a mess of trout
>
> She took them home to Grandma
> She said, "Oh Grandma, dear,
> Please cook us up a pan of trout
> While Grandpa drinks his beer."

In this poem written almost forty years ago you can learn quite a bit about the Mongins'.

Ed loves a good drink, has a playful sense of humor, and has spent his life bringing home the bluegills – or venison, depending on the season.

Teresa is also well-represented as a great cook, a magician in the kitchen, and the generous woman at the center of Ed's world.

She invested her entire life as a labor of love to build their family, foster their home, and nurture relationships with every one of us so that we keep coming home year after year.

In a patriarchal world, my grandmother built a matriarchy and taught all of us – even my grandfather – that strong feminine energy can build a community of people who genuinely care for one another and constantly show up for each other.

Every single one of us, without exception, is smart, talented, thoughtful, innovative, courteous, courageous, and kind. We've all gone to different schools, lived in different places, and led very different lives. But there are two people we all have in common: Teresa and Edward Mongin.

This isn't a coincidence. They are sources of inspiration, generosity, kindness, forgiveness, and the kind of connection that transcends generations. This little book is intended to share some of that inspiration with you through Ed's poems and the stories behind them.

In part one of this collection, you'll read poems Ed wrote for Teresa during their 60-plus years of marriage. You'll be taken on a journey through their milestones and missteps, and along the way, you'll see the love that has kept them – and our family – connected through all this time.

In parts two and three, Ed will introduce you to their circle of friends, family, and community through poetic storytelling. My grandfather's words will capture the beauty of friendship, the elegance of time, and the life lessons he's learned along the way.

My grandparents are extraordinary people who have had a powerful impact on the people around them. They've taught me to have faith, be grateful, and to create your own miracles along the way.

These are the values that came into play after Ed's accident. So, as a family, we put forth our own prognosis – one more positive, hopeful, and aligned with the iron-clad will of the grandfather. We know that true happiness and health comes from within because Ed wrote about it long ago.

> *Happiness only comes from you,*
> *From where you are and that what you do.*
> *Be like a river that gathers and grows.*
> *Don't take you for granted, like fingers and toes.*

Like a river, Ed ebbed and flowed in his recovery, but he ultimately walked out of the hospital, with Teresa at his side, within a few short weeks.

Just another reminder to never take for granted fingers and toes.

Ashley Anne, PhD
November 2023

PART ONE: LOVE

HOW I MET MY WIFE

To fully appreciate the poems in part one of this book, you really need to know the story of I, Ed Mongin, met my wife, Teresa.

When I graduated from high school, I joined the National Guard. The idea was to get my service to my country behind me to avoid getting drafted later. By joining the Guard, I'd go on active duty for six months and then return home to attend the occasional meeting. This plan allowed me to work in the family business. All went according to plan. By January 1961, I was back working with my dad.

Shortly after I settled into my new routine, the Berlin Crisis broke out in Germany and the whole U.S. National Guard, 32 Army Division was called to active duty. I was immediately sent to station in Fort Lewis, Washington – half a country away from my small hometown in Wisconsin.

It didn't take long for me to meet a man who would end up being a lifelong best friend: Dumbo. His real name was Ron, but someone pointed out how his ears were as big as Dumbo the elephant, so it didn't take us long to thereafter forever call him Dumbo.

Anyway, Dumbo was planning to marry his high school sweetheart. The wedding was scheduled to happen during our upcoming Christmas leave back in his hometown, only eight miles away from my own.

Another soldier friend of his was supposed to be Dumbo's best man, but decided at the last minute to back out. He'd met a girl in

Washington and wanted to spend Christmas with her. Time was running short and Dumbo needed a best man. He decided I was his next best option, partly because I was an easy last-minute addition since I lived in the area, but also because we were becoming good friends.

I was a bit skeptical, but he insisted by saying his fiancé, Judy, had a best friend, Teresa, who was beautiful, unattached, and would be matched with me as maid of honor. He said I'd be a fool not to help him out, so I agreed.

This is the pivotal point that set into motion the rest of my life.

I met Teresa at the wedding rehearsal and she was everything Dumbo promised and more. We hit it off right away and by the end of our first night, I managed to steal a kiss or two.

We were together for most of the little leave time I had left. Then it was back to Washington for me, and Teresa had to finish high school. That's when the letter writing began, and we really got to know each other.

Although she was a timid 18-year-old who had never been more than 50 miles from home, Teresa persuaded her father to allow her to get on a bus the summer after she graduated in 1962. Her brother, Dean, was going to college in Missoula, Montana. Although she had told everyone she intended to visit him, she had other things on her mind.

Once she arrived in Missoula, Teresa convinced Dean to take her to see her friend Judy in Washington. I think she may have mentioned me at that time as well, but in any case, she made it clear she was not finished with her cross-country trip and kept going until she reached me in Washington.

Although I lived in the barracks on base, Judy and Dumbo lived in an apartment so Teresa could stay with them. Dean returned to

Montana and left Teresa in Washington. Thank goodness for good brothers.

We had about a week, and we made the most of it. Dumbo and Judy let us use their car, and whenever I could get off base, we were together.

We went to Puget Sound to see the Pacific, up to Seattle to the World's Fair, checked out the recently-built space needle, and drove to the top of Mt. Rainier where we had to stop the car to let a grizzly bear pass while driving back down.

Then sadly, it was time for Teresa to get back on a bus to head to Dean's in Montana. When she arrived, he was nowhere to be found and the house was locked. She was sitting on the front steps deciding what to do next, contemplating breaking a window, when Dean's landlady walked up. Teresa explained her plight and the landlady invited her to stay at her home until Dean returned.

Teresa had been feeling guilty that she hadn't asked Dean to stay a while in Washington and go with us to the World Fair, but as it turned out Dean had his own agenda. He went out to visit his new girlfriend at the time and that's why he wasn't home when Teresa returned. Both Teresa and Dean met the loves of their life in the summer of 1962.

Once Teresa returned to Wisconsin, our letter writing continued on as the Berlin Crisis melted away. I had hoped to return home soon, but we got word that the Russians had planted missiles in Cuba, so my stay in the army continued on a few months longer. By October 1962, I was finally back home to Teresa.

My earliest recollection of our courtship is having told Teresa I'd pick her up for church Sunday morning. Needless to say, I overslept.

I hopped in my car and put the pedal to the metal, making the seven-mile trip in less than five minutes. I saw Teresa walking down the sidewalk, having entirely given up on me, fuming because I hadn't followed through.

As I pulled up beside her, a state trooper pulled up behind me. Teresa took one look, shook her head, and kept right on walking.

The officer didn't buy my story of being fresh out of the army and being late to pick up my girlfriend. He also said he'd been chasing me the entire time and had me clocked at 95 miles per hour. I honestly had no idea he was even behind me. So, he wrote out the ticket and was on his way.

Teresa being the wonderful person she is, laughed, forgave me, and still allowed me to accompany her at church.

Teresa and I continued to date for another six months with an engagement shortly after. We fell in love and got married while still too young to realize what we were doing. She was nineteen and I was twenty, and we were head over heels in love with each other. We were also very unaware of what laid ahead.

Teresa was a Tammy Wynette, *Stand by Your Man*, selfless kind of girl and I was a work hard, party hard, selfish kind of guy. When I wasn't working, I was hunting or fishing, and if I wasn't hunting or fishing, I was probably in a tavern. In other words, we were not terribly compatible. What we did have in common was our Catholic faith and the family we would eventually create.

Our marriage led to five children. I felt my main responsibility was to make the money and to be the bad guy when the kids misbehaved. This left Teresa paying the bills, cleaning the house, making the meals, washing the clothes, taking care of the kids, and working in the office of our business. In other words, Teresa was greatly overworked and underpaid.

We never stopped loving each other though, and each and every poem shows that to be true. I like to think my poems became the glue that helped hold our marriage together. They were my way of saying sorry for something, asking forgiveness, and because Teresa is who she is, she always found a way to demonstrate understanding and forgiveness.

Along the way, there were many good times. Teresa loved to play softball and was the team's star shortstop. After the games we would celebrate the wins or losses at the bar that sponsored the team. Those were great times, drinking beer, laughing and dancing, she loved to dance.

There were also hard times, perhaps the hardest of which was when I had a heart attack at 42. Teresa got the scare of her life at one of the kids' ball games when Boomer (another lifelong friend with a well-earned nickname) and Dumbo rushed in to tell her what had happened.

By the grace of God, I survived the heart attack, and the two following heart bypass surgeries at the ages of 49 and 68. I credit Teresa for my health today because she was always there for me. She is by far the best nurse a man could ever have, which she demonstrated time and time again.

One year, I came down with pneumonia while at deer camp and ended up in a very small hospital in a very small town. The nurse would come into my room, give me something for the pain, and then return to take my temperature and do it all over again. At the start, I had pneumonia in one lung, but by the end of the week, it spread to both. The hospital team finally panicked when my temperature hit 107, so at that point, I finally called in the big guns: my wife.

I don't know who she talked to or what she said, but before long I was in an ambulance headed to Green Bay. Once there, a specialist got things turned around and in a couple of days I was

FIRST BAPTIST CHURCH

Asst. Pastor Stephen Peel

"Glorifying God passionately through loving obedience to Him and to His Great Commission."

Sunday School: 9:45 am; Sunday Morning Worship: 10:45 am
Wednesday: G.R.O.W. 6:00 pm; THRIVE 6:00 pm; Prayer Meeting 6:00 pm

March 3rd, 2024
Communion Sunday

Message by Bob Woulf
Philippians 4:21-23

This Week (Mar 4 - Mar 10):
Deacon: Dan Sopata
Deaconess: Susan Gross
Trustee: Mike Kempka
CE Board: Christie Copiskey
FCS Board: Tim Banaszak
Missionary: Ramos Family
Member: Dan & Peggy Sopata

Events:
Mon:	Deacon Mtg.	6:00 pm
Tues:	Trustee & Deaconess Mtgs.	6:30 pm
Wed:	GROW	6:00 - 7:30 pm
Wed:	THRIVE	6:00 - 7:35 pm
Wed:	Prayer Mtg.	6:00 pm
Thur:	Ladies' Bib. St.	6:00 pm
Fri:	SOS Escape Rm.	4:00 pm

Upcoming Events:
Mar 27: THRIVE Escape Rooms
Mar 29: Good Friday Service
Mar 31: Easter Breakfast
Apr 20: Ladies' Event

DAYLIGHT SAVINGS TIME
We spring forward bright and early next Sunday morning, don't forget to change your clocks so you're not late for church!

SOS ESCAPE ROOM AND DINNER
This Friday, SOS will have an Escape Room and Fish Fry dinner at the church at 4 pm. Please sign up in the hallway to attend and if you're able to bring some of the food! If you have questions, reach out to the Pagels, Wilsons, or Brands.

THRIVE MESSIANIC SEDER
Our Messianic Seder presentation is tonight! We are excited to have a guest come share with us what the Passover Seder elements mean in regard to our Savior! See you at 6 pm if you signed up. Students helping set up, please be here at 4:30 pm. We will have dinner for the students setting up, but the presentation for everyone will only contain samples of the elements, so plan to eat before.

3014 Business 141, Pound, WI 54161; 920-897-3678
Website: firstbaptistpound.net   Email: office@firstbaptistpound.net
Secretary Office Hours: Tuesday and Thursday 8 am-3:30 pm

Statistics for Feb 25th, 2024

Sunday School	103
Morning Service	139

Regular Offering:

Feb. 25th	YTD:
$5,646.30	$42,206.19

Capital Fund:

Feb. 25th	TTD:
$0.00	$36,093.36

Nursery Schedule (0-2 Years):

This Week:

S.S.	Marcia T. & Susan G.
A.M.	Jody & Cayse G. & Bailey K.
Wed.	Edie T. & Pam T.

Next Week:

S.S.	Paul & Megan M.
A.M.	David & Tiffany H. & Leanna G.
Wed.	Beth T. & Valerie N.

Children's Church (3 yr - 1st Gr.)

Please pray for the Sopata family as they mourn the loss of Dan's father, and the Gusick family as they mourn the loss of Gerry's brother.

FIRST BAPTIST CHURCH EASTER CHOIR

The Easter Choir will rehearse after the morning service on March 3rd, 10th, 17th, and 24th. If you still haven't decided if you want to participate, please feel free to show up to the first rehearsal to see what you think! If you have any questions, feel free to reach out to April!

HELP PROOFREADING COOKBOOK

Danielle is looking for 5-7 ladies who are willing to help proofread the cookbook on March 14th at church beginning at 1 pm. She'll probably have pie to snack on since that's pi day. :) It's preferred if you have a laptop you are able to bring, but she will have a couple extras. It's possible to use your phone, but not as efficient. Please text her if you're willing! 715-291-8891

EASTER FLOWERS

If you are interested in ordering Easter Flowers in honor/memory of a loved one, please sign up in the hallway by March 17th! The flowers will decorate the stage for Easter morning and then you get to take them home. Prices are as follows:
4" Crocuses or Hyacinths -- $10
4" Daffodils or Tulips -- $12
6" Tulips -- $18
Easter Lily -- $20
Questions? Talk to Sherrie W.

THRIVE ESCAPE ROOMS

We are taking students to Green Bay for Escape Rooms and Chick-Fil-A on Wednesday, March 27th! The van will leave FCS at 4 pm and return around 8 pm. Kids should bring $20 for the escape room plus money for dinner. Please talk to Pastor Stephen or Lydia if you have any questions!

Hebrews 13:17
Obey your leaders and submit to them, for they are keeping watch over your souls, as those who will have to give an account. Let them do this with joy and not with groaning, for that would be of no advantage to you.

out of the woods. On that occasion and many others, Teresa saved my life.

In truth, I owe Teresa much of my life and am grateful for all the times she stood by my side, forgave my missteps, and supported our family.

I never thought about it until now, but the glue must have dried around our forty-second anniversary because it seems the apologetic poetry and professions of love seemed no longer necessary.

> *The love we have now is a far cry*
> *From that what brought us together.*
> *Sixty years have now gone by*
> *Our love is stronger, wiser, and a whole lot better.*

When reading these first poems, know that you will be walking, if just for a moment, in Ed and Teresa's shoes.

IN ALL THE SONGS OF SOLOMON

In all the songs of Solomon
not once did he compare,
to things that match the
beauty of your legs or breasts or hair.

For there is nothing to describe
your beauty here on Earth
a heavenly delight
I see a being of priceless worth.

TERESA'S LOVE

Your love is like the rain in spring that melts the winter's snow
That turns the grass from brown to green, and makes the flowers grow

For when it flows into my heart, in things you say and do
Just like the grass and flowers grow, my life begins anew.

And when the suns of summer shine, your love is in them too
Warming up my very soul, with things you say and do.

When the frost of autumn comes and leaves are falling down
The beauty of your love reflects the colors that abound

And in the quiet beauty of a snowy winter night,
A love that's just as true and pure, as winter's snow is white.

A love my actions seldom thank and yet I hold so dear,
A love that I can feel and see, all seasons of the year.

I LOVE MY WOMAN

I love my woman.
Love her all the time.
Older though she gets
Vintage like the finest wine
Endless are the times
My love makes my heart sing
Yesterdays have come and gone
What will tomorrow bring
Oh may she forever
My love always be
And keep a place in her heart
Never far from me.

Love you,

Ed

IT TAKES A LOT OF WATER

It takes a lot of water
To make a flower grow.

It takes a lot of living
To learn the things we know.

It takes a lot of giving
For the little we receive.

It takes a lot of trusting
In the things that we believe.

It takes a lot of praying
To our Father up above.

To make this life worth living
It takes a lot of love.

I love you.

Be mine, Valentine.

Ed

WHEN THINGS ARE BAD

when things are bad and you're feeling blue,
and everything you say or do,
seems to come out wrong and then
you start to feel much worse again
take the time to think of me
whose love you have eternally
the guy you've been with 15 years
whose laughed your laughs and shared your tears
whose goal in life will always be
to love and share his life with thee

love always,

ed

ALL GOOD THINGS TAKE TIME

All good things take time, they say
Like making love, you know
Time to be the best they can
Time and room to grow

You've given me so much of you
Nineteen years of love
Understand my many faults
I thank God above

That even when I let you down
You forgive and love me more
How can I explain to you
How much that I adore

What you've done for me
Through all the years gone by
To keep us here together now
I do not question why

But rather choose to look ahead
At where I am going to go
Only with you will I ever find
The time and room to grow

WE MAY BE AS DIFFERENT

We may be as different as day and night
As opposite as wrong and right
But we're still together

What would a day be without the rest of night
Or would a world be without wrong and right
No matter, we're still together

What really matters is that we care
Not the common things we share
And I love you, more each day
In a very special way

Because we're still together

I STOPPED TO THINK TODAY

I stopped to think today,
we've made it twenty years somehow

as many years as we had lived
we've been together now

twenty years of having kids
living day by day

trying each to be ourselves,
yet searching for the way

to keep two different people,
together somehow to stay

suddenly I realized,
we must have found the way

OUR LOVE IS NOT A STAGNANT POND

our love is not a stagnant pond,
where waters never flow
but rather like a giant pine
that took long years to grow

through years of cold and wind and drought
whose roots went ever down
until it had a hold on life
that's seldom ever found

and now sits back and waits the dawn
of every passing day
knowing that whatever comes
its strength will find the way

LOTTERY TICKETS

I thought about diamonds
Flowers or candy
Emeralds or Rubies or Pearls
Would be dandy
But I know what you like
And I sure want to please
And so, for your Valentine
I bought you these

Me

THE MONKEY GREETING CARD

A note to say I'm sorry
For things I did or didn't do
For the times I've made you unhappy
Or hurt you thru and thru

Each day we spend together lately
I realize more and more
Just how much you mean to me
It's you that I adore

So when I do a stupid thing
Like I did last night
Somehow I have to let you know
I want to make it right

A flower isn't much to give
I hope it tells the story
Of just how much you mean to me
And let's you know I'm sorry

I sure can be a monkey sometimes.

I love you,

Ed

BE MY VALENTINE

way back then
when we said I do
we never knew what
we'd go thru
some things good
and others bad
sometimes happy
sometimes sad
often during the
course of living
doing things that
needed forgiving
thru it all we're
still together
I love you just
as much as ever
I loved you then
and I love you still
I love you now
and I always will

Ed

I LOVE YOU IN THE MORNING

I love you in the morning
All day into the night
For all the times I'm wrong
And you're so very right
I love you for putting up with me
For so many years
I'm sorry for the times
I cost you so many tears
Please know I love you all the time
Please say you'll be my valentine

Me

TWENTY-FIVE

For the twenty-fifth time
You've said no presents please
For twenty-five Christmases
And twenty-five trees

Some have been calm
And others have been wild
And now we've been blessed
With our first grandchild

And this is the year
Our family alone
Will share Christmas Eve
In our very own home

For the twenty-five years
That you shared by life
I've had no greater gift
Thank you for being my wife

TWENTY-SEVEN

It took a lot of love
and God above
and laughter and tears

To stick it thru
for me and you
for oh so many years

It was two and four
and a whole lot more
and now it's twenty-seven

A marriage that
we know in fact
was sure not made in Heaven

But I'm sure glad
for the time we've had
for the laughter and the tears

You've done your part
right from the start
as the days turned into years

And I want you to know
that I love you so
and if some way somehow

It is god's will
I'll be with you still
twenty-seven years from now

I'VE BEEN LOOKING

I've been looking for a Valentine
That would somehow let you know
How much I love you for what you've done
Through the years we had to grow

I know they've not been easy
I know I've made it hard
You've always been there through it all
I can't find the words on any card

So let me say it on my own
Without the hearts or frills
You've been there on the rainy days
You've raised the kids and paid the bills

You've sat up nights and worried
And wished that I was there
You trimmed the tree and hid the eggs
While I was who knows where

You cut my hair and cured my ills
Your patience has been never ending
For the tears you've shed because of me
This valentine I'm sending

Love ya,

Ed

TWENTY-NINE

the sun doesn't always shine
the seasons don't arrive on time
the moon shines full then goes away
it rains in January snows in May
thru twenty-nine years of nature's quirks
thru twenty-nine years of joys and hurts
one thing has remained constant and free
that's the love that you have given me
a better wife I could not find
to be with for another twenty-nine

I love you,

Ed

I WANT YOU TO KNOW

I want you to know
You're on my mind all the time
Especially today
Please be my valentine

I love you,

Ed

THIRTY

Teresa,

Thirty years come and go
Things keep changing as we grow

What once was black and white today
Seems to come in shades of grey

Forgiveness now comes much more easily
What once were storms are now less breezy

Life continues to rock the boat
But somehow we stay afloat

We look back and find a way
Then go forward day by day

Our tested love has gotten stronger
Each day together we are longer

Love ya always,

Ed

TO PLUCK A ROSE

Love's a word often acclaimed
and yet a word hard to explain
the what the why the reason for
that make you the one, that I adore
often not, the words aren't there
to tell you just how much I care
so let this flower speak for me
in its beauty let you see
the thing in life that makes us mourn
are not unlike the rose's thorn
to pluck a rose, one must take care
fully knowing that the thorns are there
I love you for what I see
the budding flower on the tree

A QUIET TIME

So that you could have a special Valentine,
I wrote a special poem *A Quiet Time*.

As I lie beside you, in the dark of night, my dear
Though sleepy eyed and tired, one thing is crystal clear

That all the things that came, between us dear today
Have vanished with the daylight, you've made them go away

By taking time to hold me, and showing that you care
My hope goes on eternal, that we will always share

This special time together, in the quiet of the night
That lets me know tomorrow, everything will start out right.

Be mine forever,

Ed

SOMETIMES INSIDE I FEEL ALONE

Sometimes inside I feel alone
Waiting for your loving touch
Always searching for that smile
Or the word I need so much

Knowing that I'm often wrong
In many things I say and do.
Hoping you can understand,
The need inside I have for you.

I feel that as years go by
We realize we've missed so much.
Hoping time has made us wise
That what we seek's not out of touch.

Looking back's not always wrong
For we have much to gain
Let us not walk on separate paths
In the years that yet remain.

THIRTY-TWO

It was thirty-two years ago today
That our wedding bells did ring
We looked ahead to the happiness
We knew that day would bring

Had we known what laid ahead
And what would be said and done
As sure as we're alive today
Those bells would have never rung

And yet, who said it would be easy?
Who really has it made?
We both knew so many
Who never made the grade

And we've had some good times
With children we were blessed
The heart aches and the head aches
Whoever would have guessed?

We never gave up on each other
We always stuck it out
Because we knew what commitment
Is really all about

When one gave up on something
With frustration and despair
The other always picked up the load
And showed how much they care.

So maybe if we'd looked ahead
It wouldn't have been so good
So many things have happened
That really never could

And we wouldn't have each other
To help each other grow
Maybe God knew something
That we didn't know

Love ya always,

Ed

THE TRUNK OF A TREE

A marriage can be
Like the trunk of a tree
If it's allowed to grow.

With a crown from above
To nourish with love
And the roots doing the same from below.

A trunk that can weave
And bend with the breeze
While anchored in solid ground

By roots holding fast
To what really lasts
Committing to not falling down.

Broken branches like tears
That fall through the years
Becoming knots that strengthened the wood

That keeps the two one
When all is said and done
Looking out for each other's good.

As the roots grow on down
Away from the crown
The crown reaches up to the sky.

Though further apart
Close in their heart
Their trunk is the reason why.

A marriage can be like the trunk of a tree
Joining two like roots and a crown.

If allowed to let grow
To hold on or let go
Whether reaching upward or down.

Love ya more each year,

Ed

YOU DON'T ASK WHY

When you love someone
You don't ask why
You just do

You laugh when they laugh
Cry when they cry
Feel for them when they're blue

I know how hard
You work for us all
Not thinking at all about you

And sometimes when
We're all having a ball
We forget about what you do

So I'm telling you now
As best as I can
To let you know how I feel

You're my superstar
I'm your greatest fan
And my love for you is real.

Love,

Ed.

TERESA BE MINE

I love to watch you scratch a card
To make a buck you work so hard

I love to watch you take a nap
Or hide your hair in that crazy cap

I love you summer, winter, fall, and spring
I love about you everything.

Ed

FORTY-TWO

Forty-two years is a long long time
But I can still tell you in words that rhyme
How much I love you dear

I can remember yet
The first time we met
You didn't even like beer

But I sure liked you
And you liked me too
And I just want to say

The way you made me feel
That I was special, for real
And I still feel it today

And that's why I say
I love you today
Through the laughter and tears

In words that rhyme
After a long long time
After all of these forty-two years

PART TWO: FRIENDSHIP

BILLY AND HIS 394

Gather around boys and I'll tell you
Once more
About hot rod Billy and his 394

He was down at the race track early
In the morning
Practicin' for the race next day

He put her in first and let out the clutch
And 394 was away

He was going down the track doing
50 miles an hour, when he threw her in
Second gear

And all you could hear above the roar
Of the engine
Was a high-pitched squeal from the rear

He had her wound up tight when he
Hit that corner
He reached for that lever once more

But that was the last shift, the very last slam shift
For Billy and his 394

He was going around the corner doing
90 miles an hour
His tires broke into a squeal

They found him in the wreck with
His foot on the throttle
His hands clutched tight to the wheel

Let there be no sorrow let there be no pain
For Billy boy didn't die in vain

He always said, got to go someday
And when I go
I want to go that way

With the engine a-roaring and
The big wheels turning and me without
A care

Cause I've got just one race
One last big race
Waiting for me up there

Story pg. 112

PETER THE PLINK

Peter the plink
a bit of a dink
when it comes to the Schlida award

Cut up Ed
with a poem he read
thinks he's sharp as a two-edged sword

But he's about to find
when it comes to rhymes
he may have met his match

For it's time for him
to sink or swim
in the cleaning fluid batch

He gave a yank
as he turned the crank
he had cleaning fluid galore

He stood in a trance
and it ran down his pants
and out on the concrete floor

A five gallon can
he held in his hand
as he turned on the pump

Ten gallons he tried
to put inside
as he slipped and fell on his rump

As if not aware
that it soaked up his hair
to his feet he quickly rose

Then looking around
with a bit of a frown
wiped the dripping fluid from his nose

Needless to say
for the rest of the day
Peter was very mean

And all could tell
cause he smelled like hell
he was also very clean

Story pg. 113

HALF OVER

Thru misty eyes
We realize
Our lives are now half over

Our dreams of youth
Give way to truth
There's more to life than clover

We've felt remorse
Or talked divorce
Friends and parents dying

As kids leave home
We feel alone
There's days and nights spent crying

Our hair turns gray
What? We say
The list is never ending

Nature's way
To convey
The message that she's sending

So we've been told
We're growing old
Does that really matter?

It's crystal clear
That's what we fear
But wouldn't you really rather

Stop looking back
Get on track
You've still got a way to go

Look instead
To what lies ahead
Spread your wings and grow

Put away your fears
And dry your tears
Look forward to each day

Forget the past
The best is last
God planned it that way

You've led the horse
And set the course
Your battles are mostly won

It's not the end
You're born again
Your second half's begun

Story pg. 114

THE REUNION

Once again together
Birds of a feather
Coming from near and far

To share a meal
Talk about how we feel
What we were and what we are

We thank God we're here
Drinking soda and beer
And take a moment to bow our head

Remembering they
Who have passed away
Peter, Jim, Ruth, Roger, and Fred

Bless this our meal
Keep our love real
Help us to do your will

Show us the way
To be happy with gray
To live full lives until

We gather together
Birds of a feather
In five years, wouldn't it be nifty

If we can all be here
Drinking soda and beer
Fifty years for the class of Sixty

-Story pg. 114

50 YEARS

We now know how fast
time can fly
since we left school
a half century went by

I was thinking back
to long ago
and though there was one thing
my grandchild should know

So I took him out back
under a tree
and sat him down
upon my knee

And told him stories
of when I was a lad
about what I did
and didn't have

Like that our toilet
was outside out back
a two-holer
in a wooden shack

And I know more than one
if you get my meaning
where the Milwaukee journal
wasn't just for reading

Child, our water
came out of a pump
and when my father spoke
I'd better jump

When the phone rang
one was for you, two for me
the other neighbors
were four and three

When you heard it ring
wait a time
there were no secrets
on a party line

No refrigerator
at that time
an ice box
would do just fine

And everyone
had a favorite show
to listen to at night
on the radio

The Shadow Knows
or *Amos and Andy*
and if Ma made popcorn
that would be just dandy

No television
or microwave
what? no, my child,
we didn't live in a cave

But it was different back then
when I was a lad
life was slower
and not all that bad

So keep this in mind
as you grow

it's not what you have
I want you to know

Happiness comes from inside
and what you do
Grandpa lived without things
and so can you

Story pg. 114

THE DEVIL'S PLAN

The devil had a plan
To bring a parish down
Split up the people
Living in two towns

Divide and conquer
A ploy that he knew
Had worked well for centuries
And would work now too

He'd be sure and give them
Reasons to fight
And cloud from their vision
That there's more than one right

And when with their fighting
It would cost them a priest
It certainly wouldn't hurt
His plan in the least

For a flock without Shepard
Is quickly disbursed
He chuckled to himself
As he thought of the worst

Meanwhile in church
Back at the ranch
The bishop had Thomas
Out on a branch

Being one himself
It would take a Polish man he knew
To leave a good job
And jump back in that stew

So he pushed, God pulled
The branch gave a creak
And Sir Thomas Mayfeski
Made his gallant leap

Back to St. Francis
And those that he loved
His own life could wait
A new call from above

To teach us that answers
Are there when you search
That there's more than a building
When you're speaking of church

He used common sense
Tempered with love
And motivated the people
With a word or a shove

He brought us together
And showed us the light
That in every situation
There's more than one right

That working together
For what's best for all
Is what God expects
It's everyone's call

Take a close look around you
And be sure what you see
Would not have been possible
Without Father Tom Mayfeski

Story pg. 115

ODE TO ANNETTE

An ode of regret
For the loss of Annette
Of the finest and serious kind

Would be hard to write
If I took day and night
For the verses would be hard to find

And so better still
I think that I will
Throw serious things to the wind

And concentrate how
She's been, up until now
Kept people from thinking she sinned

Now I'll not be the one
To say this flying nun
Ever fell off of the wall

But many's the time
She's been walking the line
It's a wonder that she didn't fall

However calling to mind
All of the time
She's put in for all of us here

For her own good of course
She must ride her horse
Or partake in a bottle of beer

For how can you preach
Or take time to teach
What you know nothing about

This life is to live
And to share and to give
And to take from within and let out

And no one I know
Continues to grow
From the zest that comes from within

Better than she
An example for me
To fight for what's right and to win

And the love that we feel
For this nun is so real
That even in verses that rhyme

This ode of regret
For the loss of Annette
Is the finest and serious kind.

Story pg. 115

SISTER DONNA

To put in words what Donna has is no simple task for me.
Her virtues are as numerous as the fish are in the sea.

The treasures that she leaves for us are as countless as the stars.
Like raindrops falling from the sky, a busy freeway's cars.

Her simple smile and loving eyes, the dimple on her chin.
Her caring heart and gentle ways that warm you from within.

Her happy spirit that bubbles forth like water from a spring.
She puts a nightingale to shame when she begins to sing.

Her strength that comes from being sure she has done what's right.
Her willingness to try again if ever she loses a fight.

Her stubbornness to push you on, good humor, and sharp wits.
That keep you at your best even when you'd like to call it quits.

In the time she's spent with us she's shared our joys and tears.
She taught us how to know ourselves and helped us with our fears.

An island in an ocean.
A harvest moon on high.
A flower in the desert.
A rainbow in the sky.

She stands alone, a special friend to all within her reach.
God help you, Donna, to never change.
You practice what you preach.

> Story pg. 115

SISTER CHERYL

She's many things to many people
A church within, without a steeple
One sent from God to help us grow
Though hard for some to get to know.

While others know she's open sharing
Always listening, always caring
Always friendly, pleasant, glowing,
Smiling, knowing where she's going.

But not so fast as not to see,
A flower budding or a tree.
For in all things she takes delight,
A morning sun, a moon at night.

An open heart with deep affection
Who's taught us how to seek perfection.
She looks so young, and talks so old
She gave so much and now we're told

She has to leave, it's time to go
So she can help some others grow.
These words were written so she'll know clearly
That each of us will miss her dearly.

Love and sharing are her game,
Sister Cheryl is her name.

Story pg. 115

AMY

I've said it before
and I'll say it again
when Romy found Amy,
he found a gem.

No shiny diamond
or pearls of lace,
can match the sparkle in her eyes
or smile on her face.

First to come, last to leave
when there's work to be done.
Putting everything in place
while we're having fun.

A good man deserves a good woman,
the two become one.
A very special couple
when all's said and done.

BOOMER'S IN A PLACE WHERE

There's no more sorrow, no more pain
No more lost in the rain

No more arrows in the hand
Walk with Dumbo, scout new land

You can go where you want to go
And leave no footprint in the snow

Take your time, you can rest
Where there's neither East nor West

In loving memory of Boomer.

Story pg. 116

FRANK

friendships that last
through years apart
once again kindled
in mind and in heart

by something as simple
as liking to fish
sadly remembered
in times like this

brook trout, bluegills,
and bismaroons
card games played
in smoke-filled rooms

stories to tell
and then retold
back in the cabin
out of the cold

I put you in charge
of the young guys that day
and somehow they managed
to lose their way

and you found yourself
in a bit of a pickle
while they sang karaoke
at the Wooden Nickel

so you called the cabin
Ed, what shall I do?
Frank, I put you in charge
that's why I picked you

I'm not sure how he did it
but it wasn't long after
the boys were back at the cabin
in good humored laughter

we had lots of fun
as much as you can
Frank, this camp's going
to miss you, man

In loving memory of Frank.

Story pg. 118

MISSING THEM

No more to launch the old canoe
In beaver dams or lake or slough.

Nowhere to hike days hot or cold
To secret spots where trout grow old.

No time left to chase the bucks
Or ride the trails in beat up trucks.

Our friendships will not be forgot.
Knowing them has meant a lot.

They'll be with us still in stories told.
They'll know the secrets heaven holds.

They've went to check the ins and outs.
We'll follow soon. They're the scouts.

In loving memory of my good friend, Fred and all the people I fished or hunted with who are gone but not forgotten.

DEBBIE AND KEN - A LOVE THAT NEVER ENDS

Ken said, Debbie, I love you, you're most important in my life.
Debbie said, Ken, likewise
I'll be glad to be your wife.

She said, We'll work together.
He said, I'll be your sword.
We'll live our lives together
And share it with the Lord.

We thank him for each other
For our love and for our health.
Even though we're always broke
It's hard to count our wealth.

Our wedding will be special
But it will only last a day.
Our marriage will go on
Through sunny skies and gray.

We'll cling to what's important
Our family and our friends
And show the world around us
A love that never ends.

You said it, and I know you can do it. - Ed

Story pg. 119

ED AND ROSIE FISHIN'

To catch a pail of bluegills
Was our only mission
Back in June of '86
When I took Rosie fishin'

As I rowed along the shore
We caught fish among the logs
Bluegills nearly every cast
And bass along the bogs

I taught her how to feel her bait
As I rowed the boat
Take up the slack and watch the line
And you won't need a float

She snagged a log and cussed it
And I said, That won't do
But did the same when I unhooked it
Because I broke her pole in two

She said, You think I'm kidding
But really it's not a joke
These fish are biting much to fast
I don't have time to smoke

An eagle soared over head
A loon let out a wail
And as we reeled in two more fish
A beaver slapped his tail

He fooled us for a moment
As we shared a secret wish
That the splash had been made
By some gigantic fish

And as the stars began to light
And replace the setting sun
We made our way back to the car
Our day was rightly done

And now I'm caught in winter's grasp
And find myself a wishin'
For a day like the one
When I took Rosie fishin'

Story pg. 120

PART THREE:
LIFE

LIKE A RIVER

Two arms and two legs
Ten fingers and toes
Are taken for granted
Everyone knows

Except if you lack them
How important they be
Everyone has them
Why not me?

You can search for a lifetime
Log many a mile
To find what you're seeking
You had all the while

What makes you happy
Is not what you lack
Or where you've been
There's no sense looking back

It's what you have now
And where you are going
That's what God gave you
And how you are growing

For too often we look
At others and see
All that they have
Why can't it be me?

As they look at us
And wonder what lies
Behind all we have
They lack in their eyes

For every person
That God put on Earth
Has a special mission
To find their own worth

To know that they
Can give others a lift
By being themselves
They're one of God's gifts

Happiness comes
Only from you
From that what you are
And that what you do

Be like a river
That gathers and grows
Don't take you for granted
Like fingers and toes

SEPTEMBER 11TH 2001

September 11, 2001
Osama Bin Laden, what have you done?

You high-jacked our planes, invaded our skies
Took down the world towers, and all of those lives.

To millions of people, you brought grief and trouble
Reduced concrete and steel to ashes and rubble.

The victims are many, survivors are few
Whether Christian, Hindu, Muslim, or Jew.

You put fear in our hearts where once there was truth
Over 3000 angels now watch over us.

To help our leaders that you put to the test
To finally unite the East and the West.

September 11, 2001
Osama Bin Laden, what have you done?

You defied Allah and Islam all good Muslims know
Then hid in the ground like a rat in a hole.

You upset the masses, to a few you're a hero
To the rest of the world, just a rich zero

Whose cowardly ways are a threat to all races
With you in the world, there are no safe places.

So we're coming to get you, you'll know when we're near.
Over 3000 angels above you will hear.

September 11, 2001
Osama Bin Laden, what have you done?

And when this is over, a long while yet I fear
We all will be closer than we were that first year.

All countries, all races, all many, yet one
United together by this evil you've done.

A world better off, united in love
Guided by angels, and God up above.

Good and harmony replacing evil and fears
Peace in the world for the next hundred years.

September 11, 2001
Osama Bin Laden, you've made the world one.

I CAME TO SEE

I came to see
I knew not why

Somehow I knew
I had to try

And what I found
And what I feel

Is hard to believe
It's really real

The love of God
Is so alive

There is no place
That I can hide

No longer can I turn away
From what I always knew

That there is so much more
For God that I can do

St. Peter's table gave me strength
A rock I'll always be

To spread the word of God to all
By really being me

JOYCE'S HEART

Listen carefully
To my voice
When you asked for hope
God sent you Joyce

For nearly
Ninety years
She taught you how
To live with tears

How to handle
Grief and sorrow
Grieve today
Live tomorrow

Live each moment
Love each day
Smell the flowers
Along the way

Greet those you meet
Like sisters and brothers
Think less of yourself
And more of others

When God sent her
He knew from the start
She'd be a very small woman
With a very big heart!

Story pg. 121

MONGIN FAMILY PRAYER

Thank you, Lord for a brand new day,
For arms and legs that work and play,
For friends and neighbors near and far,
For cats and dogs and horses and what we are,
Help us to be the best we can
To see you lord in our fellow man
To know you better and live your way
Lord Jesus Christ for this we pray.

Story pg. 126

MOODS

Moods we have, like a flashing light
Are sometimes dark, sometimes bright

Often times it seems so true
That others have more than you

That life's unfair, there is no room
For anything but dark and gloom

But truly nothing is unfair
It's the devil's wish that we compare

For that's the way you fail to see
The light that shines inside of thee

Knowing what we are, that we're alright
Takes the dark away from the flashing light.

PARENTS' NIGHT

Parents are people, but oh so much more
Too special for words to explain

You've fed us and clothed us and care for our health
You gave us our life and our name

We welcome you here in the spirit of thanks
For all of the things that you do

For getting us to our practice and games
For caring and just being you

Tonight we'll play the best that we can
We'll give our all to win

But if we lose, we'll not be down
For losing is never a sin

It's how you play the game that counts
Life's game is never done

With parents like you, we're proud to say
That the game is already won

LISA

I watched you as a little girl
With pride I always knew
You would be the very best
At everything you'd do

You always did it your way
All the while you were growing
No one had to lead you
You knew where you were going

We butted heads so many times
I'm stubborn just like you
You and I are much alike
I guess that's why I knew

That whatever you chose to do in life
You would be the best
No matter what you had to do
You would pass the test

You've worked hard to get this far
There's nothing you can't do
You're sure to make it all the way
By just being you

That's what makes you so special
You stand out in a crowd
Just as you did as a little girl
You make your father proud.

Love you – Dad

Story pg. 122

TINA'S GIFT

Oh God gives every one of us
a special kind of love.
He sends it down from heaven
on the wing tips of a dove.

It's always something different
and it comes to you and me.
When Mom and Dad conceive us
and it's what we're meant to be.

When God sent it to Tina,
he must have thought a while.
To give her those big brown eyes
and oh, that special smile.

He must have thought of all the good
that he had ever done.
And wrapped it in a special gift
and let her be the one.

That he would give this special gift
this special kind of love.
He sent it down from heaven
on the wing tips of a dove.

It's always something different
and it comes to you and me.
When Mom and Dad conceive us
and it's what we're meant to be. □

Some of us get outer strength
for others it's within.
My Tina has so much of both.
She runs just like the wind.

Her love for everybody
shows in all she does.
She makes the most of what she has
and knows it's all because

God gave her a special gift
a special kind of love.
He sent it down from heaven
on the wing tips of a dove.

It's always something different
and it comes to you and me.
When Mom and Dad conceive us
and it's what we're meant to be.

I know she'll have a child
of her own someday.
And hope that she'll be blessed as I
in some special way.

She always shared her gift with me
which makes me very glad
For what God gave to Tina
and that I am her dad.

Story pg. 122

ANNIE REA

Annie-Rea you're special
You're faster than a deer
You dribble down the floor with ease
And shoot without fear

You're as pretty as a flower
You smile a special way
You've been patient with your father
And waited for this day

So sweet sixteen my butterfly
I now must let you go
To flitter through the skies of life
To spread your wings and grow

No longer will I say, No
When you want to have a date
But remember it's still up to me
To let you know how late

And I'll still be around
To lecture when you're bad
To tell you what to do or don't
Or I wouldn't be your dad

But remember that I love you
I only want what's best
We only have a few years left
You may be gone the rest

You always were so tiny
And now how much you've grown
It's hard for me to forget
The baby girl I've known

So if someday you break a wing
As you flitter through the air
Come to me I'll patch it up
Your problems I will share

And when you're happy tell me too
So your joy we both can share
Hold my hand from time to time
And join me in my chair

And always remember
Even when you're gone from home
If you ever need me
You'll never be alone

You'll always be my baby
You mean so much to me
Of all the folks I've ever known
You're special Annie-Rea

Story pg. 122

TRENT

We were told
we could write a letter
but we thought
that a poem might be better.

To let you know
how a little boy
came to our home
and brought great joy.

He got into
his teacher's hair
and was then
kicked out of daycare.

He came to stay
with us each day
and we got
to teach him our way.

Cans were crushed
and sausage made,
and there was no trap
that made you afraid.

In the red wagon
to the park you did ride
picking up leaves
with Grandma at your side.

Breakfast with Florence
brought you good luck
because before it was over
she'd give you a buck.

And later in life
the fun that we had
hunting and fishing
with you and your dad.

And stories we told
remember the one
when all that we heard
was the click of the gun.

So as you grow old
remember your past
let Jesus be
your first and your last.

We'll say it often
and we'll say it loud
you, young man,
have made us **PROUD!**

Written for our grandson's confirmation.

A FAR AWAY WEDDING WISH

People ask who you are
We say Mercedes but not a car

A top-of-the-line girl is she
A graduate from MIT

She's super smart and daughter grand
Who lives in a far-off land

With kangaroos and wallabies
And koalas in Eucalyptus trees

Today is her wedding day
And all that we wish to say

Is we miss you much and wish we were there
We hope you know how much we care

May God grant you as husband and wife
A long and healthy, happy life!

Written for our granddaughter, Mercedes, who found and married the love of her life in Australia.

LIKE YOUR MOTHER

what can I say?
there is nothing that can make this go away

when it comes to love
there is no other
that can love you
like your mother

she never cared what you did or how you lived
she was always there to forgive

she always loved you in a way
that you knew you could never repay

I'm sure she's looking
down right now
trying to figure out
just how

she can take your
hurt away
and bring sunshine in
to your day

to let you know
there is no other
who still loves you
like your mother

Written for our step grandson whose mother passed away when he was quite young.

RAINDROPS AND RAINBOWS

My grandpa said
I'm old and gray
But there's something
I want to say

I love you child
I've watched you grow
You are a woman
And now you know

Someday soon
You'll hold someone's hand
And then there will be a
Wedding band

You'll have good
Days and nights
And some awful
Dragged out fights

Remember child
What your grandpa knows
It takes raindrops
To make rainbows

You'll have some children
This I know
I hope I live
To see them grow

They'll be both
Good and bad
They'll make you happy
And sometimes sad

Remember child
Your grandpa knows
It takes raindrops
To make to rainbows

As life goes on
You'll face new tests
Always try
To do what's best

Weather each storm
That comes your way
Tomorrow is
A brighter day

Remember, your grandpa knows
It takes raindrops to make rainbows

Story pg. 123

THE WHALE

As my daughters grew
All of them knew
Someday, they'd have to listen to me

Tell them about men and boys
With their trucks and toys
And how they are as numerous as fish in the sea

Not the first one you see
Not a dozen maybe
Will be the one for you

Take a long look
Study them like a book
Before you decide on who

What first makes you happy
Can turn out quite crappy
As time goes on by

Know what they do
Watch how they treat you
If there's something you question, ask why

Some people learn slow
But that's how you grow
Now you grandgirls listen to me

I want you to take note
Before you get in that boat
There's a lot of fish in the sea

Tina was smart
She'd had a head start
She knew what she was looking for

No bullhead or carp
Would get to her heart
Someone special could open that door

And when Mark came along
Like in a love song
It was a fisherman's dream come true

She put the sea in pail
and pulled out a whale
Tina, we're so happy for you.

Story pg. 124

TURNING FORTY

For many a year
You've dreaded the day
When you would be forty
And people would say

Your best years are gone
You're over the hill
You've given your man
His very last thrill

Your hair's falling out
Or at least turning grey
You're lucky if you
Can get through the day

But think for a moment
And I'm sure you will find
That you're at your best
It's not the end of the line.

For isn't it older
Women they say
That make better lovers
By night and by day.

And now that the kids
Are beginning to leave
Wouldn't you have more time
To do as you please?

The best years I'm sure
Must lie ahead
So cheer up tonight
You've nothing to dread

Look around closely
I'm sure you will find
That those who aren't forty
Are not far behind

THE PERFECT THIEF

Who's the villain, the robber, the perfect thief.
It's the passing of time, that's my belief.

Fifty-five years, what can I say?
Too many of us have passed away.

He's taken our eye sight, our hearing, our hair
And a few other things we're not willing to share.

And leaving us little of what we once were
But what we have going is what I prefer.

To dwell on for now in the time that remains
To count up our blessings and add up our gains.

Children and grandchildren, great grand for some,
Battles with finances or health, problems won.

We're smarter and wiser; we're taking our pills.
We're ready for whatever; we've written our wills.

We're living each day and giving him grief.
We're staying one step ahead of the perfect thief.

Story pg. 114

LEONE'S POEM

I was blind, but now I see
No walker, pain, or pills for me

Let my passing bring you smiles
I now can walk a hundred miles

I'm with Pa and Cheryl and Dean
You wouldn't believe the things I've seen

Now I can be with you, whenever you wish
At a party or when you fish

Whole again, a risen soul
The greatest gift you'll ever know

I was blind, but now I see
No walker, pain, or pills for me

Written in loving memory of my mother.

Story pg. 125

A LOOK IN THE MIRROR

I look in the mirror and what do I see
An old man, looking back at me.

I say to myself, that can't be
So I look again - yeah, that's me.

But the mirror can't see inside
There's more to me, I have my pride.

I can no longer run up a hill
But I can make it up there still.

If I walk and sit and walk and sit
Until I'm to the top of it.

And getting down is a piece of cake
If I don't fall and my bones don't break.

I can still get in a boat
And in my old canoe a river float.

And when I shoot a buck and it's time for bragging
I call my grandson to do the dragging.

So being old, maybe it's not that bad
When I think of all the fun I've had.

And the fun I'm having even still
You only have to have the will.

So look in the mirror but do not hide
Look beyond to what's inside.

Story pg. 114

MY LAST PRAYER

Lord

Death is a passing
from my world to thine
My only regret
are those left behind

I've longed to be with you
for so many years
Give them some gladness
to go with their tears

May they see in my death
the way that I lived
May they know that I gave them
all I could give

Let them know tomorrow
they too must pass over
That only through death
can we walk in the clover

That grows in the valleys
of your heaven above
There we'll share with each other
your infinite love

Amen

Story pg. 127

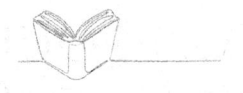

PART FOUR: STORIES BEHIND THE POEMS

SURPRISE

To say the least I was pleasantly surprised when I was handed this book of poems that I had written over many years. I knew my wife had kept some of them but not this many. She had shared them with my daughter and granddaughter and my granddaughter had them published in this book.

As I read over my work it came to me that although the words mean much to me, to anyone else a lot of them are just words that rhyme. Every poem either has a story or tells a story. If you don't know the story you can't fully appreciate the poem. It was after that realization that I decided to add the stories that go with the poems.

I share this first poem that I composed with my father as an example of what I mean. I was about 10 years old at the time and we were driving home from a fishing trip. We had a bucket of fish, more then we really wanted to clean. At the end of our street lived an elderly widow woman with her two elderly daughters all of which did not like to fish but didn't mind cleaning them and very much enjoyed eating them. Their last name was Duprey and so this poem was born. My father and I enjoyed reciting it many times after our fishing trips. Fun fact, this poem was never written down anywhere but kept safely in my mind until now. It goes like this:

Duprey girls here we come,
Bringing you some cleaning fun

From the fish we have to spare
We are bringing you your share

You may have them all for naught
This string of pan fish that we caught

If but a contract you will sign
Saying you'll take them all the time.

BILLY'S STORY

Billy's Story – page 54

I wrote this as a song about my best friend at the time.

It was the 1960's and we were always street racing with someone. Billy loved working on cars to make them ever faster. The 394 was a 1953 Studebaker with a 1959 Oldsmobile 394 engine.

None of this song ever happened. It's purely fiction, and Billy is still alive and well today. I haven't seen him for a while but I wouldn't be at all surprised if he's still burning rubber.

PETER'S STORY

Peter the Plink– page 56

This story has two parts.

My brothers and I owned several auto parts stores and Peter was a long-time employee and friend.

Each year at our Christmas party, we'd pass along what we called the Schlida Award. It was a trophy of a horse's behind that was passed from one employee or owner to the next for the funniest mess up of the year.

This year Peter knew he was going to get the award, and that I would probably write a poem about it. So, he decided to beat me to the punch by writing one of his own about one of my mess ups that year. This poem tells the rest of the story.

REUNION POEMS

Half Over – page 58
The Reunion – page 60
50 Years – page 61
The Perfect Thief – page 105
Look in the Mirror – page 107

This collection of poems was written for my high school class reunions. I launched my career as class poet with *Half Over*. It was well-received, so the rest of the poems followed suit.

The Perfect Thief was originally written for 2020 but as many other things were shut down so was our reunion. We didn't meet until 2022 so it sat in wait until then.

Look in a Mirror tells my own story of aging.

THE STORIES FOR OUR CHURCH

The Devil's Plan – page 64
Ode to Annette – page 67
Sister Donna – page 69
Sister Cheryl – page 70

In the late 70's and early 80's, our church diocese was experiencing a shortage of priests, so parishes needed to be combined.

Our town and the next were only two miles apart and were to be some of the first to merge. This led to a lot of contention. A new church was to be built to accommodate the consolidation and, of course, we wanted it in our town and the other town wanted it in theirs. A neutral site was discussed but none of the discussions were going anywhere.

Father Tom had been the priest prior to the talk of consolidation and was well-liked by the people of both parishes. He had moved on and was replaced by a priest that was a native to our community. This did not help matters in the least. As the discussions failed and frustration grew higher, the bishop turned to Father Tom for help.

I was the chairman of the building committee and served on the parish council. I loved the people of both towns and worked hard alongside Father Tom to bring them back together. There are many stories I could write about this time in our history but that would take a whole other book.

It's enough to say it all worked out in the end. We had a lot of help especially from the sisters that were assigned to the parish. Sister Annette and Sister Donna were there during the worst of it and Sister Cheryl came along after the worst was over. They were all very special people who helped make the wonderful parish we have today. "The Devil's Plan" is about the battle and the Sisters' poems were written for their going away parties.

BOOMER'S STORY

Boomer's In a Place Where – page 72

This poem was my closing words at my best friend Boomer's funeral. I recited them after I told the following stories.

He was a very special friend who loved to hunt and we would spend nearly every day together during deer season, both bow and gun. He got his name when we were hunting ducks with friends. Whenever a duck flew overhead Boomer would fire two shots, boom boom. By the end of the day everyone was calling him boom boom. That later morphed into Boomer or sometimes just plain Boom.

As much as he liked to be in the woods, his sense of direction was really poor. If he didn't have a compass, he was lost. One time he got mixed up and didn't show up at the car when he was supposed to. I had to go find him and it was down pouring rain. When we got back to the car my young son piped up and said, "We had a problem dad!"

"What's that, son?" I asked.

He said "Our Boomerang didn't come back!"

"Yes, you got that right."

Another time while bow hunting, Boomer accidentally shoved an arrow through his hand. While taking him to the hospital, our other good friend Dumbo stopped at a tavern.

Boomer, very excitedly, asked "What are you stopping here for?"

Dumbo replied, "You don't think I'm going to drive all the way to the hospital without a beer, do you?"

Actually, I was hunting on a different farm with Boomer's two boys and the plan was to meet at the tavern after the hunt. Dumbo was just stopping to let the owner know what had happened and where they would be. Well, maybe he stopped for both reasons.

Dumbo passed away about a week before Boomer. Two very good friends gone too soon.

The last story I shared was about Boomer and my son, James, who was about ten at the time. They were out scouting and had gotten on the wrong side of a property line. They saw a truck coming and ducked down in the brush hoping they wouldn't be seen. The land owner saw their tracks in the snow and stopped his truck, got out and started tracking them down with gun in hand.

James whispered to Boom, "Is he going to shoot us?"

Boomer replied, "I don't know, but we're gonna find out pretty quick!"

As it turned out the farmer was pretty understanding and they all had a good laugh.

I tell these stories in remembrance of one of the best friends I have ever had. We enjoyed each other's company for many years and I miss him every day.

FRANK'S STORY

Frank – page 73

Frank and his wife, Orrie, lived next door to Teresa and me back in the 1960's. We bought the home we still live in today from them. We became close friends, and Frank and I often fished together and would sometimes catch big bullfrogs known as Bismaroons.

In time they moved away to another town and we lost touch for years. One day he walked into a restaurant while I was there eating breakfast. We began talking about old times. We discovered we were both retired and we ended up rekindling our long-ago friendship.

He started coming up to my cabin and became part of my fishing camp crew. He continued coming until the day he passed away in a car accident. I told our story and wrote and recited this poem at his funeral. Frank is sorely missed.

DEBBIE AND KEN'S WEDDING STORY

Debbie and Ken – A Love That Never Ends – page 76

I met Ken when he was about 18 years old. Teresa and I were on our way to our cabin with another couple and a van full of kids. We were about 2 miles from the cabin and the fuel pump went out on the van.

I was able to locate a fuel pump and Ken volunteered to install it. It was the beginning of a lasting friendship. When he met Debbie, they shared with me their expectations and wedding plans and I wrote this poem for their wedding. They didn't disappoint me and have been happily married for 38 years now. They framed their poem and it hangs in their home to this day.

ED & ROSIE FISHIN

Ed & Rosie Fishin – page 77

Jerry and Rosie were very good customers of mine. We sold auto parts and they installed them. Our business relationship turned into a friendship, and I invited them up to my cabin in northern Wisconsin.

Boomer and I took them to one of our secret lakes in the Upper Peninsula of Michigan. We had to carry our boats into the lake that was quite a distance, and I'm sure Rosie, not at the time a diehard fisherwoman, was wondering if this could possibly be worth it.

The poem tells the story of the fishing trip, and how much fun we had. But I find the rest of the story most interesting.

I had given her the poem right after I wrote it, and she had the only copy. I'd seen Jerry many years later and he told me she still had my poem.

When we first started working on this book, I decided to go see Rosie in hopes that she still had the poem to add to our collection. Not only did she still have it but it was in her office pinned to her bulletin board with at least a thousand pin holes in it where notes had been placed over the years. She kept this poem for 37 years. The paper was yellowed and full of holes but still readable.

This one is the perfect example of the power a poem has to keep memories alive.

JOYCE'S STORY

Joyce's Heart – page 86

Joyce is my sister-in-law and Teresa's oldest sister, all four feet eleven inches of her. Her family was going to have a party to celebrate her upcoming 90th birthday.

Teresa said, "Ed, you have to write a poem for Joyce."

I asked what she wanted me to say and she said I would think of something. As I thought about Joyce, the one thing that kept coming to mind was the strength and resiliency she showed handling the loss of so many of her loved ones.

She lost her best friend in a car accident they were in while still in high school. She lost a son and grandson to car accidents, a son and son-in-law to heart attacks, and her husband to a fatal illness.

She may be small in stature but she is big in heart and love for family and life. She has taught many of us what it means to have true faith. I recited this poem to her and her family at that birthday party.

OUR CHILDREN

Lisa – page 90
Tina's Gift – page 91
Annie Rea – page 93

I wrote a poem for each of our children when they turned 16. We have five wonderful children, but we were only able to find three of the poems. Lisa is our oldest daughter, full of spunk and built to take the world by storm and she has done just that. Tina is our second child born with a lot of feelings and a big heart. Ann is our third child born with a lot of talent for many things including athletics and has found her place as a school counselor. Her nickname growing up was Annie Rea. Hint: don't call her that today unless you want to rile her up.

James is the next in line and our only boy. He has grown into an amazing man and we spend much time together fishing and hunting. Dawn is our fifth child born with a love for all things nature. She also enjoyed hunting and fishing with our crew and she has grown to be a resilient strong woman.

Teresa and I are very proud of all of our children.

RAINDROPS AND RAINBOWS

Raindrops and Rainbows – page 99

This is a poem that any grandparent can recite to their granddaughters whom somehow, overnight, magically turn into beautiful young women.

This poem was actually written as a song that two of my granddaughters put to music. I hope you find your own music in it.

THE WHALE STORY

The Whale – page 101

Being a fisherman, my daughters and granddaughters always have to put up with me comparing boys to fish. Don't fall for the first one you see, they're not all keepers.

Tina's first marriage gave us three wonderful grandchildren, but it wasn't meant to be. Then she found Mark. I wrote this poem and recited it at her second wedding.

LEONE'S POEM STORY

Leone's Poem – page 106

Leone was my mother. She passed away on my wedding anniversary two weeks before she would turn 95.

I recited this poem at her funeral and truly believe she gave me the words through the Holy Spirit to comfort all of us who loved her to let us know she's more than ok.

She was an amazing woman. We miss her and think of her often.

FAMILY PRAYER STORY

Mongin Family Prayer – page 87

This poem written many years ago became our family prayer.

Cats and dogs were in the original poem, and horses were added by my children and grandchildren who raised and loved their horses.

Whenever we get together as a family, we hold hands and recite this prayer before we sit to eat our meal. At the end, I usually add a comment of loving gratitude to Teresa for cooking.

When the accident happened, the one my granddaughter described in the beginning of this book, the doctor told us that I had a severely broken neck and if I lived through the surgery I would never walk again. Seven days later I was not only alive but walking.

I believe that this prayer, being recited by our family for so long, not asking for anything but thanking God for simple things like, arms and legs, was the reason that God intervened when that tree fell on me. I believe the reason why I'm walking is simple, when we pray God wants us to know he listens.

MY LAST PRAYER

My Last Prayer – page 108

I don't remember writing this poem, so it may have been written when I was in the hospital.

I am sure I wrote it though, because it sure sounds like me.

As of now, 2023, I'm still here.

ABOUT THE AUTHOR

Edward Mongin lives in Wisconsin with his beloved wife, enjoying his days hunting, fishing, and spending time with family and friends. He is a father, grandfather, great grandfather, and forever a poet at heart.

This collection was compiled by Ed's wife, Teresa Mongin, and edited by his granddaughter, Ashley Anne, PhD with significant contributions from Ed's daughter, Tina Marie.

Made in the USA
Monee, IL
14 January 2024